HEART OF DORKNESS

The Collected Dork Tower, Volume III

by John Kovalic

DORK STORM PRESS

OTHER BOOKS BY JOHN KOVALIC:

Dork Covenant: The Collected Dork Tower Volume I
(Issues 1-6 of the comic book)

Dork Shadows: The Collected Dork Tower Volume II
(Issues 7-12 of the comic book)

Heart of Dorkness: The Collected Dork Tower Volume III
(Issues 12-17 of the comic book)

Livin' La Vida Dorka: The Collected Dork Tower Comic Strips, IV
(Previously uncollected comic strips from national magazines & dorktwoer.com)

Wild Life: The Cardinal Collection
(Comic strips for the University of Wisconsin Daily Cardinal)

The Wild Life Journals
(Comic strips from the State Journal)

The Wild Life Files
(Comic strips from national syndication)

Dork Storm Press
PO Box 45063,
Madison, WI 53744
http://www.dorkstorm.com

Marketing, sales and advertising inquiries:
sales@dorkstorm.com
Phone: (608) 255-1348 • Fax (608) 442-1528

Editorial and other inquiries:
john@kovalic.com.

Cover design: John Kovalic & Phil Reed
Interior design and layout: Aaron Williams

PRINTED IN CANADA • FIRST PRINTING, MAY 2002 • ISBN 1-930964-43-9

To the best friends
I could ever have,

my brother
and sister.

Introduction
By Michael Stackpole

Harrumpphhhh.

Okay, it's official. I am jealous of John Kovalic.

It's not just the fact that he's a really nice guy with that "aw, shucks" boyish charm. It's not just that he has a lovely wife or lives in a cool city and that he has great taste in restaurants. (If you have a meal with him, let him pick the place.) And it's not just that he's patient and thoughtful with friends offering ideas for strips or in long conversations that range over a variety of subjects.

Nope, nope, and not even the fact that he's won an Origins Award for fiction, which I have never done.

It's really the two other things that put it right over the top for me.

The first is his art. Take a look at the opening two page spread originally from Dork Tower #13. It is wordless, save for the last panel, and yet there is no doubt that something serious is unfolding. Oddly enough, even in that last panel the words are presented more as a graphic element than anything else. Without them, we'd still know Matt was stunned, not angry. That ability to communicate mood and emotion graphically is the soul of brilliant cartooning, and John is a master of it.

Another aspect of John's incredible ability as a cartoonist that is just magnificent--and you get to see it displayed here brilliantly--is that he can shift gears and present running stories, single page strips, four panel strips and single, stand-alone cartoons. Toss in the illustrations he does for various projects in the gaming field and we're talking the cartoonist Pentathlon. ("Now accepted the Gold Medal is John Kovalic.")

(And, yes, that could sound hyperbolic, but truly isn't, and I know that in reading the above John was saying, "Oh, goodness, this is too much." See previous reference to "nice guy" and "aw, shucks.")

Okay, the biggie for me to be jealous about--nuts, even typing this becomes hard--is John's writing. I've done novels, games, short stories, columns and comics, so I kind of know my way around writing. Writing for comics is a specialized artform because the whole graphic element provides you a new toolkit with which to work. If a writer isn't sharp, opportunities to do some really great stuff slip by.

John, of course, is very sharp. I point to the Ren Faire story, third page, second panel as an example. In the background we have Ken, Igor and Carson roaming by, providing the proof to Matt's punchline. It's subtle and funny, makes a reader go, "Oh, yeah, I hear you, Matt," and provides just a bit more sympathy for Matt, who could use all he can get at that point. A lesser writer would have missed putting that graphic element in, making the whole panel just perfect.

That's just a piece of what makes John's writing great. Aside from his ability to shift gears from long stories to shorter pieces, each which comes with its own demands and challenges--once again leaving me in awe--John has got a critical ear for cosmic truths and a delightfully wicked satirical sense.

Throughout Dork Tower you can find nuggets of truth that ought to be enshrined--or, at least, force-fed to high school kids before their lives are hopelessly warped. Igor's saying, "People who wouldn't be caught dead in a bad movie or ill-fitting clothes will go months or years with the wrong person!" is simply stunning. That's one of those comments that can spark hours of great discussions--alas, discussions likely lost on those who spend more time choosing their clothes than their companions.

The satire in Dork Tower just has me smiling and chuckling throughout my reads. John sees the faults and foibles of the whole fan-boy subculture, and is able to tear off riff after riff that makes me laugh and, on occasion, blush. The Iron Chef piece not only skewered the show, but it cleanly nailed the pseudo-culinary artistry to which we resort when we have more things in the house for flavoring food, than we have food that needs to be flavored. (And it took me back to my earliest days in the industry when I proved, definitively, that one could not improve the taste of Campbell's soup by adding Spam. Or vice versa.)

The Post 9-11 strips did still manage some satire, about gamers, the net culture and even the culture of data-mongers (I can no longer bring myself to think of them as "news outlets" since all we get is raw streams of data, sometimes layered with faux-analysis by reporters who don't have time to do any research so don't really know what they're talking about). More important than that, however, is that the strips reveal depth and heart and express so eloquently the devastating emotions we all shared after that horrible day.

If you have never read Dork Tower before and just happened upon this collection, you are lucky indeed. If you are a fan of Dork Tower, this is more and better. Be ready for stories that will make you smile and laugh, that will tug at your heart strings and even make you think.

Yes, I'm jealous of John Kovalic, but as long as he keeps providing the wonderful stories of Dork Tower, I'll bear it happily.

Mike Stackpole
Phoenix, AZ
02/02/2002

Michael A. Stackpole is a New York Times best-selling author of award-winning science fiction and fantasy, including Star Wars and Battletech novels. He is also an award winning game designer, computer game designer, and great guy to bum around the American Southwest with.

"High above the muckey-muck castle made of clouds, there sits Wonderboy, sitting oh so proud..."

- Tenacious D: "Wonderboy"

14

I'VE GOT A DATE! I'VE GOT A DATE! I'VE GOT A DATE! I'VE GOT A DATE! I'VE GOT A DATE!

18

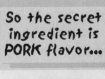

So the secret ingredient is PORK flavor...

ALLEZ CUISINE!

The challenger is known mostly for his work with macaroni and cheese, so this should...

Fukui-san?

Yes?

We're looking over the Iron Chef's shoulder to get a peek at his ingredient selection!

And what is it?

Tom-Yum paste...

This is a surprise!

Oooo! I LOVE its look! (giggle)...

...and Rice Wine and Soy Sauce, of course...

Oooo! I LOVE its look, too! (tee-hee)...

Plus Sesame Oil and...is that... FISH SAUCE?

(GASP!)

So he's a fan-boy, but ALSO an EPICUREAN with interests in ALL things Eastern...

Fukui-san?

Yes?

We've spotted the challenger's ingredient selection!

And what is it?

uhhhhh...

Generic Turkey Dogs.

So he's a baboon?

Or a college student. Sometimes it's hard to tell the differ...

I HEARD THAT!

Fukui-san?

Yes?

Iron Chef Ramen Noodle has added two cups of Water, the Pork Flavoring and the Noodles!

Giggle

He brings it to the boil, and now simmers it, adding one tablespoon of Tom-Yum paste and half a cup of Rice Wine!

Interesting...and a few frozen peas...

Fukui-san?

Yes?

Now the Iron Chef is adding a tablespoon of Soy Sauce, a tablespoon of Fish Sauce and one teaspoon of SESAME OIL...

How is it that an average fanboy has these ingredients on hand?

Iron Chef is a fan of all things Eastern. It is not uncommon for such an otaku to store such condiments in his closet!

Where we also found such DVDs as "Sailor Naked Moon," "No Time for T-Shirts" and "Naughty Tentacles of..."

HEY!

Whoops. Iron Chef has grabbed a Ginsu Knife. Time to check in on the CHALLENGER...

The Challenger has added one cup of water and two diced turkey dogs to the Noodles and Pork Flavor...

And now he's just letting it boil down?

Fukui-san?

Yes?

It appears so!

AND THERE GOES THE GONG OF FATE!

The Iron Chef has presented the judges with a dish of rare depth.

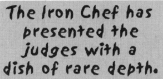

UNBELIEVABLE. SUBTLE. AROMATIC...

I DIDN'T THINK I'D LIKE THIS, BUT IT'S LIKE TASTING CLOUDS...

MUNCH MUNCH

MUNCH MUNCH

The challenger has presented... uh...GLOP...

THIS USED TO BE ORGANIC?

REMINDS ME OF COLLEGE DORM FOOD.

COLLEGE?

THE BEST YEARS OF OUR LIVES!

The battle goes to... THE CHALLENGER!

So join us NEXT time, when the secret ingredient is...

MUSKRAT!!!!

Stay tuned! Emeril turns a boring recipe into a slightly LESS boring recipe! NEXT on Food TV! BAM!

THE END!

25

CRUD.

STAR WARS: THE PHANTOM MENACE **BIT.**

JAR-JAR BINKS WAS IDIOTIC. THE PLOT WAS PAPER-THIN.

ANAKIN WAS ATROCIOUS! THE MIDICHLORIANS WERE STUPID! THE TRADE FEDERATION WAS INSULTING, DARTH SIDIOUS WAS **OBVIOUS** AND THE WHOLE THING WAS A **TRAVESTY!**

AND I WON'T BE ABLE TO GET IT ON DVD FOR **YEARS!**

OH, HOW FANS SUFFER...

Lucas: N Star Wars DVDs until 2005

29

DORK STORM

#14
$2.95

DORK TOWER

LOVE

IS

ALL

AROUND

"Are you wearing some unusual kind of perfume, or something radioactive, my dear?"

- *Dr. McCoy to Eve, in "Mudd's women."*

38

41

43

CONCLUDED next issue...

49

HUZZAH! I DON'T BELIEVE IT!

GENTLEMEN, I GIVE YOU THE **PERFECT** DICE ROLL! THE GREATEST, TIMELIEST SINGLE ROLL WE SHALL **EVER** WITNESS! **BEHOLD** THE LEGENDARY

PERFECT ROLL!

THIS IS A **ONCE** IN A **LIFETIME** EVENT! A **DOUBLE-DOUBLE** CRITICAL **SUCCESS**! THE **RAREST** EVENT IN THE **ROLEPLAYING** WORLD! AND WE **WITNESSED** IT HERE! THE ILLUSTRIOUS, IMMORTAL **PERFECT ROLL**, AND... AND...

WHAT?

YOU'RE PLAYING WITH UNMATCHED DICE, AREN'T YOU?

OH, THE SHAME

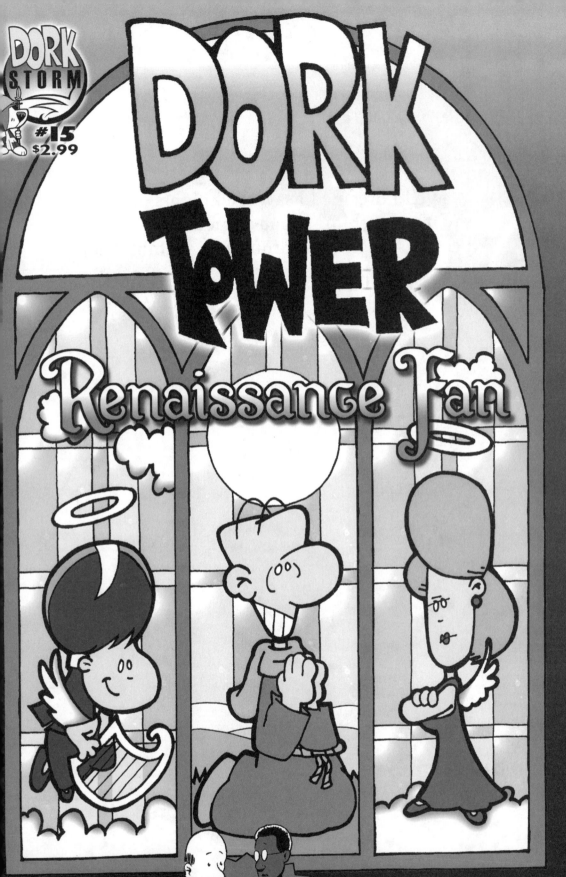

"Well I dreamed I saw the knights in armor, sayin' something about a queen. There were peasants singin' and drummers drummin' and the archer split the tree..."

- *Neil Young: "After the Gold Rush"*

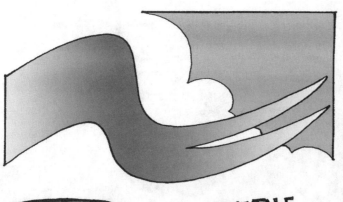

58

62

67

NOW LET'S SEE IF I'VE GOT THIS STRAIGHT: YOU HAD SO MUCH TO DRINK, MOST OF LAST NIGHT IS A BLUR.

RIGHT.

BUT YOU **DO** REMEMBER GETTING BACK TOGETHER WITH YOUR EX-GIRLFRIEND KAYLEIGH, THUS ENDING THE LONGEST ROMANTIC DROUGHT OF YOUR LIFE.

RIGHT.

UNFORTUNATELY, YOU **THEN** MET THE GIRL YOU BELIEVE COULD BE THE **LOVE** OF YOUR LIFE.

BUT BECAUSE YOU'RE BACK WITH KAYLEIGH, YOU'VE MISSED YOUR **ONE** CHANCE FOR HAPPINESS IN A UNIVERSE THAT'S ON THE WHOLE COLD, HEARTBREAKING AND **INDIFFERENT**.

RIGHT.

WHAT **HO**, MARTY! **HUZZAH!** WE'RE ON IN FIVE MINUTES! "MERRIE MINSTRELS MARTY AND TOMMY SING SONGS OF HAPPY BUNNIES" TAKES THE KIDS' STAGE **AGAIN!**

THREE MORE MEADS...

RIGHT. THREE MEADS FOR ME TOO...

ALEX ROBINSON PRESENTS

UT! IGOR, YOU JUST REALIZE YOU HAVE A TEAR IN YOUR INFINITY BAG AND YOU'VE LOST YOUR BLADE OF SLICING 'N' DICING!

NUTS!!

HAHAHA! TOUGH LUCK, OLD PAL!

OKAY: AS YOU HEAD DOWN THE PASSAGE YOU NOTICE TH--

WHAT THE--?!

LHUBBA WUMBA

STOP!! I MUST-- I MEAN, YOUNG IGOR MUST BE ALLOWED TO RETAIN HIS BLADE O'SLICING 'N' DICING!!

WHO IN THE NAME OF SMAUG MIGHT YOU BE?

I AM IGOR -- FIFTY YEARS HENCE! I'M CONTACTING YOU FROM THE FUTURE TO WARN YOU THAT IF I -- HE-- ISN'T ALLOWED TO KEEP THE DAGGER THEN THE UNIVERSE IS DOOMED!

WHAT? HOW CAN OUR GAME AFFECT THE --

POIT!

OH, COME ON! YOU'VE WATCHED ENOUGH "TREK" TO KNOW I CAN'T TELL YOU THAT!

IGOR MUST KEEP THE BLADE...

WELL. OKAY, THEN.

I PICK UP MY BLADE O' SLICING 'N' DICING AND...

WHOA WHOA WHOA, WAIT A MINUTE. WE ARE GOING TO LISTEN TO THIS SO-CALLED IGOR FROM THE FUTURE?

HOW DO WE KNOW HE'S ANY MORE HONEST THAN OUR IGOR?

I DON'T KNOW, KEN. IT'S ONLY A GAME AND FOR HIM TO VIOLATE THE SPACE/TIME CONT--

CHUB WUB

HOO-BOY. NOW WHAT?

SHERMAN! DON'T DO IT!

74

Box Office Poison characters ©2001 Alex Robinson
bopalex@aol.com • http://members.aol.com/ComicBookAlex

ABOUT DORK TOWER #15

Dork Tower #15 was published about a month after the tragedy of September 11, 2001.

The back cover was graced with Mark Smylie's poignant tribute to the heroes of New York and Washington DC. Mark, whose Eisner-nominated comic "Artesia" ran for a three-issue mini-series in Dork Tower (issues #16-18), is a good friend and a gifted artist and writer. His painting, which runs here on the inside back cover, said far more and with far greater poignancy than I could ever have hoped to.

The letters pages, review pages, free game and other backups were pulled from Dork Tower #15. In their place in I ran the cartoons from dorktower.com that were drawn in the aftermath of September 11.

The day after the tragedy, I drew the first cartoon. It took me a week to draw anything else.

All the money that came in from these cartoons went to charities that eased the suffering of untold thousands, to those that helped the victims of September 11.

Superheroes do exist in the world. September 11 showed they are all around us.

John

DORK TOWER BY JOHN KOVALIC

SEPTEMBER 11, 10 am

NUMBED AND IN SHOCK FROM THE DAY'S BREAKING TRAGEDY, I GO ONLINE.

MY E-MAIL AND MAILING LISTS ARE FILLED WITH MESSAGES OF GRIEVING AND OF HOPE. FRIENDS CHECK TO MAKE SURE I'M OK.

EVERYWHERE THERE'S A SENSE OF A COMMUNITY COMING TOGETHER, PRAYING FOR OTHERS, OFFERING TO HELP.

IT MADE ME REALIZE HOW MANY GOOD PEOPLE YOU CAN FIND OUT THERE.

AND HOW MANY WE LOST.

KOVALIC

©2001 SHETLAND PRODUCTIONS JOHN@KOVALIC.COM   HTTP://WWW.DORKTOWER.COM/INTERACTIVEWEEK.HTML

78

DORK TOWER

BY JOHN KOVALIC

Q: WHICH FORM OF DISASTER RESPONSE DO WE ACTUALLY NEED **LESS** OF?

a) HEROISM

b) CHARITY

BLOOD DRIVE TODAY!

BAKE SALE FOR RELIEF FUND MONDAY

RED CROSS DONATIONS ONLINE: 6,612,011.00

CLICK HERE TO GIVE

c) LOVE

DISASTER! NATION IN MOURNING

d) ONLINE IDIOTS

HEH. ADDING A COUPLE OF LINES TO THIS BOGUS NOSTRADAMUS QUOTE WILL **REALLY** FREAK PEOPLE OUT!

WELL, HURRY UP! I WANT TO POST BILL GATES' PICTURE ON THE WORLD TRADE CENTER "MISSING PEOPLE" WEB SITE! HAW!

SOMETIMES I **KILL** MYSELF...

HEY! THOSE NAZIS WON'T LET ME PUT WTC RUBBLE UP FOR AUCTION ON E-BAY!

KOVALIC

DORK TOWER
BY JOHN KOVALIC

1933

THE ONLY THING WE HAVE TO FEAR IS FEAR ITSELF.

2001

WELCOME TO THE 24-HOUR FEAR NETWORK. NEXT UP: 25 DIFFERENT WAYS THE TERRORISTS MAY GET YOU. PLUS, WAITING FOR THE FIRST WAVE OF E-WARFARE: WILL THEY UNLEASH COMPUTER VIRUSES OR WORMS, AND WHY WE'RE NOT READY. FOLLOWED BY LIVE-UP-TO-THE-MINUTE UNEDITED TERRORIST THREATS AND STATEMENTS. AND CHECK OUT OUR WEBSITE FOR STREAMING VIDEO OF ANTI-WESTERN RALLIES, LURID REPORTS ON EVERY MINOR JET LINER PROBLEM EVER AND AN INTERACTIVE ANIMATION OF WHY SO MANY PEOPLE WANT US DEAD, DEAD, DEAD!

PLUS ANTHRAX. BUT FIRST, WHY ARE PEOPLE SO FEARFUL? OUR PANEL OF EXPERTS TRIES TO FIGURE IT OUT...

HTTP://WWW.DORKTOWER.COM/INTERACTIVEWEEK.HTML

"I am more afraid of an army of a hundred sheep led by a lion than an army of a hundred lions led by a sheep."

- *Talleyrand*

DORK STORM PRESS in conjunction with SHETLAND PRODUCTIONS and in cooperation with LETHARGIC PRESS presents the MOST ANTICIPATED crossover of the CENTURY! The TEAM-UP readers DEMANDED! ZAP! POW! EXCELSIOR! It's...

DORK TOWER

versus

Lethargic Lad

YOU KNOW, IT'S FUNNY, BUT FOR ALL THE YEARS WE'VE LIVED IN MUD BAY, WE'VE NEVER MET UP WITH **Lethargic Lad.**

CHEZ GEEK

WARHAMSTER RALLY

THE BIG BOOK OF LETHARGIC LAD

AMAZONA, SWORDMISTRESS OF AURORA, AND HER COMPATRIOTS...

IS IT TOO LATE TO OPT FOR FOUL, FESTERING DEATH?

I DON'T NEED TO TAKE THIS, YOU KNOW! I **OFFERED** TO INTRODUCE YOU TO ROLEPLAYING WHILE KEN AND MATT WERE RUNNING THEIR ERRANDS! SO IF YOU **WANT** TO TELL THE DIFFERENCE IN HIT-POINTS BETWEEN A **HOMUNCULUS** AND A **HELL HOUND...**

WHAT'S A "HOMUNCULUS?"

WHAT'S A "HIT POINT?"

HOWSABOUT WE JUST TAKE IT FOR GRANTED I'M DEAD, AND I START ROLLING UP A NEW CHARACTER **NOW**?

NO! BY THE TIME I'M DONE WITH YOU, YOU'LL BE A **LEAN, MEAN GAMING MACHINE!** YOU'LL HAVE THE **EYE** OF THE **WERE-TIGER!**

... EVEN **IF** GILLY'S ONLY ROLE-PLAYED **ONCE** BEFORE, KAYLEIGH **NEVER,** AND AN **ENTIRE** DUNGEON OF EVIL NOW LAYS BEFORE YOU...

MAYBE MY NEXT CHARACTER COULD BE A MORTICIAN TO SAVE TIME...

SUCCESSFUL ROLEPLAYING MEANS YOU'LL HONE **MANY** SKILLS: DECISION-MAKING; PUZZLE-SOLVING; **SWEET-TALKING** THE **GAME MASTER** ...

EVEN IF HE'S A MEGALOMANIACAL LITTLE **FREAK** WHO'S LET POWER GO TO HIS **HEAD**?

DEAD, DEAD, **DEAD**...

WHAT DO YOU DO?

WE GO BACK TO TOWN.

WHAT?

GOOD GRACIOUS, YES. FOR STARTERS, JUST LOOK AT MY CHARACTER. SHE NEEDS TO BUY SOME CLOTHES!

UH... CLOTHES?

ONLY AN IDIOT IS GOING TO FIGHT EVIL IN HER UNDERWEAR.

CLOTHES, ARMOR... THIS GIRL NEEDS EVERYTHING. SHE MUST BE FREEZING!

NEVER MIND THE ORCS. AMAZONA IS PROBABLY MORE WORRIED ABOUT CATCHING HER DEATH FROM COLD.

WHAT KIND OF SICKO WOULD SEND A GIRL OUT AGAINST PERILOUS DANGER WHEN SHE'S HALF-NAKED?

I THINK SHE USED TO BE IGOR'S OLD CHARACT...

CARSON!

I MEAN HEH... HEH... UH... ER... HEH...

CLOTHES, YOU SAY...

CLOTHES.

ROLL ROLL ROLL ROLL

PLAYER HAND

AHHH. **MUCH** BETTER!

FINE!

SO GILLY ALSO GETS HER 'HOLY ARMOR' AND 'MACE OF SMITING?'

FINE!

AND **CARSON** GETS HIS 'RING OF PROTECTION FROM, FRANKLY, ANYTHING'?

FINE!

GOOD. NOW, **LATER** I'D LIKE TO DISCUSS WHY AMAZONA HAS A "BUST SIZE" STAT, TWO PAIRS OF HANDCUFFS AND ATTRIBUTES CALLED "LEATHERWORK," "KNOWLEDGE OF JELL-O" AND "ATTRACTION TO SHORT, STOUT MEN WITH LARGE NOSES"

BUT FOR NOW, WE CAN START.

FINE! SUPER! LET'S START!

YOU'RE BACK AT THE DUNGEON DOOR. OPENING IT, YOU SEE A PEDESTAL IN A SMALL ROOM. ON TOP OF IT IS THE LEGENDARY **GEM** OF **ETERNAL** POWER!

GLEE!

SO, YOU PICK IT UP, AND...

WE **SO** DO NOT!

ERR... PARDON?

WE IGNORE IT!

IG... IG... *IGNORE* IT..?

LOOK, IT'S **CALLED** THE GEM OF ETERNAL POWER, AND IT'S IN THE *VERY FIRST ROOM* WE ENTER? HOW BIG A BOZO DO YOU HAVE TO **BE** TO FALL FOR A TRAP LIKE THAT?

Twitch
Twitch

WELL, IGOR ONCE

NEVER MIND THAT!

SO... YOU PROCEED INTO THE **NEXT ROOM**...,

"THE **HALL** OF **INFINITE ORCS!**

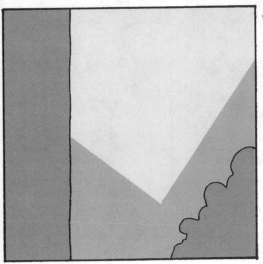

"Galstaff, you have entered the door to the north. You are now by yourself, standing in a dark room. The pungent smell of mildew emanates from the wet dungeon walls..."

"Where are the Cheetos?"

- The Dead Alewives: "Summoner Geeks"

AHEM!

GOOD DAY. IGOR OLMAN HERE.

AS YOU CAN TELL FROM THIS ISSUE'S **VARIANT COVERS**, AS WELL AS THE FACT THAT OUR LOGO IS NOW A **REGISTERED TRADEMARK**, DORK TOWER HAS NOW OFFICIALLY **SOLD OUT**. **BIG** TIME.

SO WHAT CHANGES CAN **YOU**, THE **READER**, EXPECT TO SEE IN THE UPCOMING MONTHS?

FOR A **START**, NOW THAT WE'VE GONE **CORPORATE**, DRESS CODES WILL RIGOROUSLY BE ENFORCED AT **ALL** TIMES (SAVE FOR CASUAL FRIDAYS, WHEN BUTTONED COLLARS ARE OPTIONAL).

ALSO, **DORK STORM PRESS** WILL NOW, BY LAW, BE KNOWN AS "**DORK $TORM PRE$$**" ON ALL INTERNET FORUMS.

OUR LITTLE COTTAGE INDUSTRY WILL REMAIN LARGELY THE SAME, SAVE FOR ONE OR TWO **COSMETIC** CHANGES...

... OUR NEW DIGS, FOR EXAMPLE ...

DORK STORM INC.

FORMERLY ENRON, INC.

The END

Night of the Dinner Table

114

WHO'S HUGH D. HUGH?

A NON-PLAYER CHARACTER WE ENCOUNTERED A LONG TIME AGO. IT INVOLVED A GAZEBO, A COW AND A ONE-LEGGED DWARF.

HE DOESN'T SEEM TO RECOGNIZE US AT ALL. GEEZE. YOU'D THINK HE'D REMEMBER WE ONCE TRIED TO HELP HIM...

WELL, VIOLENTLY TRAUMATIC EXPERIENCES TEND TO BE THE ONES PEOPLE BLOCK OUT BEST...

YOU TRIED TO RESCUE HIM FROM A LIFE-THREATENING SITUATION?

NO... WE TRIED TO HELP HIM CROSS THE ROAD. **DARN** THOSE CRITICAL FUMBLE ROLLS...

YOU'RE RIGHT. HUGH APPROACHES YOU, BUT DOESN'T SEEM TO KNOW WHO YOU ARE. HOWEVER, HIS **LIMP** HAS APPARENTLY HEALED, AS HAS HIS NERVOUS TWITCH, SEVERE BURNS AND UNSIGHTLY DISFIGURATIONS...

THAT'S HOW HE WAS WHEN YOU TRIED TO HELP HIM?

THAT'S HOW HE WAS **AFTER** WE TRIED TO HELP HIM.

HUGH D. HUGH!

I DON'T SUPPOSE THERE'S ANY CHANCE OF GETTING A **STIFF DRINK**, IS THERE?

YES! HUZZAH! LET'S LOOK AROUND FOR A FRIENDLY NEIGHBORHOOD TAVERN WHERE WE CAN CAROUSE **MIGHTILY!**

THAT'S NOT WHAT I MEANT...

ROLL ROLL ROLL

AM I DRUNK YET?

IS THERE A SHUTTLECOCK OR SOMETHING I COULD STRIKE HIM WITH?

127

128

> ## "Teamwork: A chance to blame someone else."
> ### - Devil's Dictionary

The Dork Tower Swimsuit Issue
Pages 131-136

The comic strips from the Dork Tower Swimsuit Special #1 (November) ran in Livin' La Vida Dorka (The Collected Dork Tower Volume IV). As I noted there, sales of this were not what I'd hoped, since I chose to title it "The Dork Tower Swimsuit Special #1" and NOT "A Whole Bunch Of Gaming-Related Comic Strips That You'll Probably Really, Really Like If You Enjoy the Regular Comic Book, plus a few Parody Swimsuit Shots from Some of my Friends."

So anyway, these are the takes some of my pals had on the Dork Tower gang. Page 132, Phil Foglio; page 133, Keith Knight; page 134, Alex Robinson; page 135, Jon "Bean" Hastings; page 136, Rich Koslowski.*

The Dragon Magazine Jams
Pages 138-140

In 2001, the Dragon Magazine annual was comi up, and editor Dave "John, have more wine!" Gro thought it would be a blast if Aaron Williams, P Foglio and I swapped comics for the issu

So I wrote and drew Aaron's "Nodwick," Aar wrote and drew Phil's "What's New" and Phil wro and drew "Dork Tower."

Dave left the magazine soon afterwards. I like to thii the two events are not connected.** But here a the results of one idea, two weeks to complete assignment and three cartoonists who obviously c not be trusted with each others' characters***

---

* Not having learned my lesson, look for "The Dork Tower Swimsuit Special #2" December 2002..
** OK. Seriously, they weren't connected. Dave left for bigger and better things, and now hangs out with people like Georg Lucas instead of me. But I'm not bitter. At all. Really. No. Really. Honest.   Uh-uh....nope...(whimper)..
*** Of course, I won't mention the time my friend Jay Rath needed me to take over his strip, "Mad Town" for a time while h was on vacation, and I KILLED OFF a character of his without his knowing, just for yuks.

FOR JOHN K

ALEX ROBINSON
·2000·

134

SUDDENLY, THE BOYS' GAME OF "CAPTURE THE FLAG" WENT HORRIBLY, HORRIBLY WRONG.

LOOK AT THOSE GEEKS!
LOOK AT THOSE DORKS!
GEEZ! THIS THONG IS KILLIN' ME!!

The DRAGON™ Jam

Phil and Dixie are ™ & ©2000 Studio Foglio · www.studiofoglio.com

140

AVAST, YE SCURVY DOGS!

It must be mine!

X 9   ♔ 9

Slash **S**
D
P

ACTION

Act: Get an unaligned Captain card (from outside your deck) and put that captain into play. Congratulations! You now have an additional Captain in play. You do not lose the game until all of your captains have been sunk. This card remains in play. If this card is ever discarded or sunk, all of your Captains are sunk as well. You may not play this card unless you are the credited artist of this card, or your name appears in the credits section of the most current rulebook or rulesheet.

"HUZZAH!" - Carson the Muskrat

In 2001, my pals at AEG asked me to do a special promotional card for their 7th Sea collectible card game. They wanted to call it the Dread Pirate Carson.

It had been years since I'd done a CCG card, and the chance to dabble in oils (THERE'S a mental image) was too good to pass up. And no Dork Tower character had EVER been on a collectible card before...

Well, The Dread Pirate Carson card somehow became the "It must be mine!" card, and almost immediately after printing deemed too powerful for actual play. So, like, six people in the WORLD have copies, most of them work at AEG, and I've lost two of my three. The third is framed, so I can't use it. And the others have been destroyed, I'm told.

I framed my copy and gave it to Judith. She gets all the good stuff.

One was auctioned by Alderac for charity (it went for $400, or somesuch).

Most of the rest are, apparently, swimming with the fishes, with Jimmy Hoffa.

Me? I love the fact that a card called "It must be mine!" is next to impossible to find...by ANYONE.

CLANBOOK:
Perky

Sun is shining in the sky, there ain't a cloud in sight
It's stopped rainin', everybody's in a play, and don't you know,
It's a beautiful new day! Hey hey!
-The Electric Light Orchestra, *Mr. Blue Sky*.

Introduction

As we all know, the undying damned and accursed are divided into clans and factions. There are many theories as to why this should be. Some say that the blood of the clan founders flows strong, warping the souls of their progeny. Some say that the curse of immortality can be assuaged by few joys, and in the absence of chocolate-flavored hemoglobin, politics is the best option going. Some, the most bold, whisper fearfully that it's a publishing thing. Actually, for those who aren't much good at fighting faction wars, arguing about why the Undead fight faction wars is a pretty big hobby in itself.

But in the annals of the Kindred, one bloodline above all is whispered of with special dread. It's not that there are many of them, or that they are particularly tough. It's just that, in a society of blasphemers, they commit the ultimate blasphemy. In an eternity of horror, they have a unique ability to horrify the horrific. In a world of transcendent angst, they transcend angst itself.

In fact, there's a nasty suspicion that they're having fun.

This is the tale of this strangest of all the Accursed, The Clan Who Wave To Their Friends, Those Who Bring Sunshine To Those Who Hate The Sun, The Ones Who Quite Like Lilac: *Clan Perky*.

Chapter 1: Eternal Cheerfulness

"It is demonstrable," said he, "that things cannot be otherwise than as they are; for as all things have been created for some end, they must necessarily be created for the best end...

– Dr. Pangloss, in *Voltaire's Candide*.

No-one knows for certain how Clan Perky was founded, or even by who. There is some suspicion that whoever it was noticed that the other founders looked neat in black (with silver jewelry), and decided to join in. How he, she, or it got away with this is another matter, but some occult

historians have conjectured that the First Per was someone's kid sister.

The Clan has been on the edges of Kindr history ever since, causing unintended troul at every turn. When Rome fell to decaden amongst wild celebrations, someone was telli Nero that his legs looked good in that short to When the Mongol Hordes swept across Chi someone was doing cute tricks with chopstic When pirates sailed the Spanish Main, somebo not only persuaded the big blond hunk to d his beard black, but talked him into tyi fireworks in it.

Today, as the Final Days and Nights are up us, as Armageddon looms and Unspeakab Monsters are spoken of more often in hush and nervous tones, as (it is said) the Day Up Which Every God Must Shave With A Raz That Is Hired is at hand... Clan Perky is mu as ever. Nothing seems to worry them too mu It really is very strange, and a bit of a pain in t anatomy. But what can any self-respecti bloodsucking leech expect, of people who t the word "moderation" when they're talki about mascara?

Attitudes (as in, Having Real)

For the members of Clan Perky are ruled forces other than passion or excess. If they of the Kindred, it is not because a ghastly f permits them no other sanctuary in a World Dimness™; it is because they think it might fun. And fun, it has been observed, is alwa optional.

In other words, at some level, Perkies do have to be here. They can take this stuff or lea it alone, but they choose to take it. Which mal them, from the point of view of the other p people in black with whom they hang o infinitely worse than those who choose to lea it alone. Because the other Clans can always fe superior to those who spurn their dark a dreadful lifestyle, but the Perkies – them, th have to live with. (Or unlive with. Whateve

So what is it that makes the Perkies contin hanging around with these miserable so-and-s who barely disguise their burning disdain f everything Perky? Well, there are a lot of answ to that. Being somebody's kid brother or sis often comes into it, and the music is sometin an important consideration. Also, frankly, not Perkies are really that alert, socia speaking, so some of them ju haven't noticed that they aren't 10C blood group of the month. On t other hand, some of the less cud ones have noticed just fine, and some kicks from winding up t other Clans. So yes, it vari

And what is it that the Perkies in the whole death-pallor a mourning-clothes shtick? That var too. Mostly, of course, it's t dressing in black. As they say,

ean, it's quite a practical color, really – okay,
u have to keep it clean of dust, but it doesn't
ow most spillages, and it goes with *everything*."
lmittedly, it's not a conventionally cheerful
lor, but who wants to have to live up to a
awaiian shirt all the time? And some folks find
easier to be cheerful if their clothes aren't
ving them migraines.

Then there's the silver jewelry, of course. It's
ssy, it's not too expensive, and you can get it
some quite perky shapes. And thirdly, there's
e make-up. As some of their coterie-mates
spect, many Perkies aren't that long out of the
ge of playing with face paints, and they like
nging with people who accept that, even if
cy do have to limit themselves to white and
ck.

And lastly, strange to say, some Perkies are a
t shy. When they find a group that is willing
accept them – and the Kindred don't have so
any friends that they feel free to reject too
any offers of alliance – they are happy to jump

ews of Other Supernaturals

As is traditional, Clan Perky are largely ignorant
out the nature, powers, attitudes, politics,
bits, hopes, fears, dietary requirements and
ist measurements of the other supernatural
habitants of their world. (This is despite sharing
at world with these beings for millennia. Some
ople just don't pay attention.) Predictably,
wever, they refuse to let this worry them.
hat they do know can be summarized in the
ual convenient bite-sized notes.

Werewolves: "Don't worry, I'm not going to
anything silly like trying to tickle his stomach,
shouting 'Fetch.' Do you think I'm stupid?
ryway, Snookums here always says he prefers
ing scratched behind the ears."

Wizards: "And it's not just marked cards?
ool. Hey, he'd look good in a top hat and tails.
u know, like in those old movies. I mean, he
oks like a good dancer."

Ghosts: "Oh, wow, do they do the thing with
e slime?"

Fairies: "Puh-leeze. All my coterie tell me that
n uncool because of that silver pussy-cat
rring, and now you're saying I've got to believe
at there's this lot at the bottom of my garden?
e you trying to make me all unpopular?"

hapter 2: The Power of Perky

Why do birds suddenly appear every time you are near?
Just like me, they long to be close to you...
- Burt Bacharach and Hal David, *Close to You*.

As with every other Clan, the dread powers of
ose who bear the name of Perky are shaped
d twisted by the nature of their distant
ogenitor. As seems to be traditional, this means
at they have exactly two sorts of special talents
at members of other Clans can't imitate, except
hen they can. In this case, the talents are
Heliocentricity and *Optometry*.

Heliocentricity

This discipline makes of the
true Perky a terror to other
Creatures of the Night. For
mastery of Heliocentricity
enables the possessor to go
forth in daylight. More or less,
anyway.

One Splodge, ☺: The
character doesn't have to
worry much about small
chinks in the curtains when
she wakes up a little before
sunset. She may complain,
although if she is also adept in
Optometry, she will probably
shrug it off.

Two Splodges, ☺☺: The
character routinely wanders in
through the front door just as the
sun comes up, without apparent
signs of panic. Although she
doesn't go out in daylight as such,
she has an annoying capacity for
acting as though it's an option.

Three Splodges, ☺☺☺:
Flashes of full direct sunlight do
not worry a character who as
advanced this far in this
discipline. (She'll hold her hands
up to her eyes or flail after her
sunglasses, but probably look *cute*
doing so, darn it.) Despite a
tendency to hang around in the
shadows (which may just be
shyness), she will have no problem
at all with any level of artificial
light. She may call heavily
overcast days "a bit dull" rather
than "pleasingly as gloomy as my
cursèd soul."

Four Splodges, ☺☺☺☺:
The character is forever going out
on distinctly cloudy-bright days.
(Of course, the mandatory black
get-up tends to look a little out of
place in daylight.) She can hold
down a regular day-job if she
wants, though she'll prefer
something indoors.

Five Splodges, ☺☺☺☺☺:
The completely insufferable
character is known to take
holidays on tropical beaches,
and has a load of cute
sunglasses and designer
swimsuits to prove it. She
doesn't actually tan – in fact,
she maintains a stylish, Goth-
credible pallor at all times,
despite going out in the sun –
but she actually seems to find

sunlight *pleasant*.

Optometry

This is the true, characteristic talent that causes other Clans to revile and secretly fear Clan Perky. For the Adept of Optometry is not merely *cheerful*; she downright makes a habit of it.

One Splodge, ☺: The character is properly gloomy and dour most of the time, but small irritations don't make it worse. She will accept useful suggestions of solutions with only a little nervous lip-biting.

Two Splodges, ☺☺: The character has got the hang of looking on the bright side, at least in relation to minor problems. Confronted with stuff she enjoys, she dives right in, and she tends to focus on this sort of thing rather than the bad stuff, if possible. (However, black does still look a bit funereal on her.)

Three Splodges, ☺☺☺: By now, the character may use Optometry to come up with a positive way of looking at any situation that has one. She has favorite colors, perfumes, bubblegum pop songs, and Saturday morning cartoons, and can talk about them without embarrassment; she makes cheerfulness look reasonable, at least on her.

Four Splodges, ☺☺☺☺: At the fourth level, Optometry can overcome the gloom-inducing effects of anything except genuinely tragic situations. Also, at this stage, Optometry becomes dangerously infectious. Other characters must use their own willpower or psychic defenses to avoid looking on the bright side when the Adept talks to them.

Five Splodges, ☺☺☺☺☺: The character can make saying "Ay vont tew trink yeur bleut" sound cheerful and normal. Situations, problems and psychic assaults that would worry even a normal person just make her smile and say "oh well, could be worse." She clearly only wears black because it looks insufferably, wonderfully classy on her. Other Kindred have to work really hard to remain miserable around her, even without her trying to cheer them up.

Chapter 3: Perky Folk

Hey, I've got nothing to do today but smile.
Danda-dando-dandon, here I am,
The Only Living Boy in New York.
– Paul Simon, *The Only Living Boy in New York.*

Clan Perky is its members. (Like, you thought it was the cat's mother?) This chapter reviews a little of what that means. (Like, you have trouble reading or something? "Clan Perky is its members" is just five words, you know). It starts by presenting the usual bunch of vaguely plausible starting characters (although we seem to have forgotten the character sheets. Oops. We seem to have been doing that a lot lately. Oh well, character sheets are for fascists. Well-known fact). Then we tell you about a bunch of historical

characters and suchlike people who were re (shock!) members of Clan Perky. Probably they weren't something else, and we are pretending to be some deranged Perky w thinks that everyone in the world who mat is like him.

(Yes, we know that's annoying, but we being annoying. It's called an Unreliable Narra and anyway, it's dead post-modern. And means it's really very cool. Trust us on th

Archetypes

Closet Perky

'Ho, Diomed, well met! Do you sup with Gla to-night?' said a young man of small stature, who his tunic in those loose and effeminate folds which pr him to be a gentleman and a coxcomb.
– Edward George Bulwer-Lytton, *The Days of Pompeii.*

Quote: *Them? They're a bit, umm, Perky, an they? No, I don't get on with them at all. No-sir-a diddly... I mean, not at all, for they repel my blacke soul, Great Prince. Cross my heart.*

Prelude: You are perhaps the most mysteri of Perkies, insofar as you don't seem to Perky at all, to first glance. You have slipped the company of a bunch of members of so other Clan, who have accepted you as one their own. Only occasionally have they noti your essential Perkiness making itself evide and you have got away with your own priv

asquerade so far.
Beyond that, we're not telling. So you're free
smirk and avoid the issue.

Concept: Your Clan denies that it
stematically infiltrates others, for any reason.
tually, that sounds perfectly reasonable; the
ea of Clan Perky being organized and scheming
ough to manage anything that subtle, let alone
its having long-term plans, is more than most
lk can accept. But the fact remains that you
em to have become an infiltrator, from the top
your perfect jet-black hairstyle to the tips of
ur lethally pointy boots, and what's more,
u're quite good at it. Well, nobody's blown
ur cover yet, anyway.

Roleplaying Hints: Whichever other Clan
u've infiltrated, you've got the style down
rfectly, whether it's lurching about in a plain
ack suit with claw-like fingernails moaning
Voe!" or flouncing around in a lurid waistcoat
etending to be artistic. Only occasionally does
ur disguise slip, as you are provoked into a
nny smile by some piece of good news, or you
d yourself humming Madonna songs under
ur breath. But you are trying to be more
reful; you think one or two of your coterie
ight suspect...

Possessions: Whatever it takes to maintain
ur cover, you've managed to get hold of it. If
ything, you may have been *too* smart about all
is; someone examining your wardrobe might
nclude that you've put some effort into this,
hich would rather blow the too-depressed-to-
re stance out of the water.

ndead Gamer

Get in the spirit of the game, and use your persona
play with a special personality all its own. Interact
th the other player characters and non-player characters
give the game campaign a unique flavor and "life".
– Foreword to the Advanced Dungeons & Dragons

Players Handbook (1st edition).

Quote: *Hey, can we get another session of that*
campaign in? Sorry, I mean chronicle. My character is
almost up to fifth, and I think we found a really neat
artifact last time. Perhaps we could play overnight?
What do you mean, "Not Again"?

Prelude: Even you do not know when you
slipped across the line from normality to Unlife.
It wasn't after that first game, certainly, for you
remember that you yawned on your way home
from that. Nor was it the day when your spending
on game supplements first slipped into three
figures in one shopping trip, for that was, you
are sure, in daylight. No, it must have been some
time later, as you dealt with the fact that you had
other things to do during the day by playing all
night, then dealt with the problems this induced
by sleeping during normal working hours. Now,
though, you have plunged deep into the depths
of unholiness. Or at least, you've got a bunch of
really cool PCs who you always talk about in the
first person.

Concept: "Obsessed" would probably be the
word, I'm afraid. Unlike some of the Accursed
who role-play, however, you do not focus on
gloom and despondency in your games; you are,
after all, a Perky. Rather, your secret state emerges
in the fact that you can and do play all night,
every night. This lets you get a lot of gaming in,
at the cost of making life stressful for those of
your fellow-players with more mortal
constitutions.

Roleplaying Hints: You don't trip over things,
you fumble your Spot Obvious rolls. You aren't
overweight, you just came out at the extreme
end of the Height/Weight Table. You don't annoy
people with you incessant gaming war stories,
you just get unlucky on your Reaction checks.
In short, you define everything in terms of games,
which means that you can remain happily
oblivious to the fact that you're clumsy, fat, and
a bit annoying.

Possessions: Faded black jeans (low
maintenance), a "Gaming is Life" T-shirt (though
you don't understand why people think it's a
joke), and of course a huge library of game-
books, a black velvet bag full of bizarre
polyhedrons, and a collection of weird black-
and-white comics by obscure gamer cartoonists.

Weekend Bloodsucker

I wish it was Sunday
'Cause that's my funday
My I don't have to runday.
– The Bangles, Manic Monday.

Quote: *Look, I know it's not really very credible,*
but I really need that weekday job. The money's good,
which means I can afford those nifty fingerless gloves I
saw last week. So see you on Saturday, okay?

Prelude: When you were drawn into the world
of Unlife, you spotted the flaw in the deal straight
away, and somehow, you managed to haggle a

to your true nature. After all, your taste is genuinely oriented towards the Kindred style.

Famous Perkies

Mozart: You saw the movie; pink wig, bad puns, irritating laugh. One of ours, obviously, though perhaps the sort who gives us a bad name with some people.

Doc Holliday: Okay, on the one hand, he was pale, skinny, and a bit scary, so he was evidently one of the Kindred (and not just ill). On the other, he was a dentist (is *that* any job for a deadly gunfighter?), and he called his gun "daisy." Perky or what?

Rasputin: Look, do we really have to explain this one?

way round it. For you, it's didn't become a full-time occupation; it's just something you do two days a week.

Concept: Don't get the idea that you don't take this Clan thing seriously. Just because you've got your priorities sorted out, doesn't mean that you don't know what's most important. For example, you do NOT work weekends, because that would get in the way of the things you take *seriously*. You clearly enjoy this stuff. You're a Perky, and it sometimes shows.

Roleplaying Hints: Always act enthusiastic, and make sure that you know all the intricate details of Kindred politics and secret history. Others meeting you at weekends should not easily guess the truth – until they try to get you to commit to something on a weekday evening. Then, you turn evasive and, if pushed, embarrassed. Once you know people enough to trust them with your credibility, you can become quite open about your divided life.

On weekdays, act fairly quiet and conventional, though you don't have to keep the weekend stuff completely secret. After all, the good thing about being balanced is that you can handle a little mockery or willful misunderstanding.

Possessions: Two completely separate wardrobes, one with an immaculate selection of black stuff, the other a lot more conventional, though possibly with hints as

Darth Vader: Dressed in black: check. Talked in a silly voice: check. Caused almost as much trouble for his own side as he did for the opposition: check. When somebody found a film showing him in childhood, turned out to have been an irritatingly cute kid: check…

Written by Phil • Masters
Illustrated by Aaron • Williams
Produced by John • Kovalic

PENUMBRA

THE SHEEP ON THE BORDERLANDS

Or: How I Learned to Stop Worrying and Love the Orcs

HOLMGREN

By Igor Olman, with Jeff Tidball

Edited by Michelle A. Brown Nephew
Gratuitous Development by John Nephew

Layout by Aaron Williams
Illustrated by Jason Holmgren and Aaron Williams

Explanatory Documents
Or: "Why God? Why?"

Dork Tower's enormous investigative and editorial staff has recently secured the following documents in relation to an ongoing investigation of precisely why all this seemed advisable at one point. The first is a chat log between parties who would remain nameless save for the fact that they use their actual names as IM handles.

> **JOHN_NEPHEW** << I don't care how many times he's called about his stupid module. Put it in the slush pile.
>
> **JEFF_TIDBALL** << I told him we were putting it in the slush pile. But somebody on MUSTELIDAE-L told him that "put it in the slush pile" is code for "barbecue the mother."
>
> **JOHN_NEPHEW** << Tell him to cry to somebody who cares. I got in this business to get rich, not publish commercially marginal labors of love.
>
> **JEFF_TIDBALL** << He calls constantly. Seriously. I hang up, the phone rings again, and it's him. And I think he's hacked my e-mail.
>
> **JOHN_NEPHEW** << What did you say his name was?
>
> *** "IGOR_THE_BARBARIAN" HAS JOINED YOUR CHAT ***
>
> **JEFF_TIDBALL** << Oh, crap.
>
> **IGOR_THE_BARBARIAN** << Well met, companions!
>
> **JEFF_TIDBALL** << ::Whimper::

The following is an excerpt from a letter by Tidball to his mother several weeks later:

I can't take it anymore. They've got me ghostwriting this moron from a place called, get this, Mud Bay. I mean, what, the good names were taken?

I swear, mom, if I didn't still owe John for lunch yesterday I'd just hit the road. Move to California. Become one of those pathetic people in Hollywood trying to get their feeble scripts made. At least then it would be warm in the winter and I could live in a box on the street.

All work and no play makes Jeff a very dull boy

Finally, this photograph speaks for itself.

Ground Rules

Welcome to *The Sheep on the Borderlands, Or: How I Learned to Stop Worrying and Love the Orcs.* Before we begin, let's get a few things straight. This is not some happy, new-age adventure gaming module. This is hard-core dungeon-crawling, and you're going to do it our way or hit the road. The rules:

• When you come to a text block that's italicized, and is obviously not a title or in a weird language like Latin, you read it to the players, verbatim.

My name is Dimfoodle. I am in italics.

If you do not read italicized text verbatim to the players, we will enter your house through underground steam tunnels and perform satanic rituals in your basement until small-minded local religious officials picket your house and your mom goes ballistic.

• Because of lawyers, Napster™ is dead and gaming material is divided into open and closed content. This entire module is open content, with the exception of articles ("a," "an," and "the," when used as adjectives) and non-ASCII characters, oh, and other people's trademarked or copyrighted material, too. This module is a satire ... violations of the Open Gaming License (OGL) are entirely intentional, and use of copyrighted or trademarked material does not constitute a challenge to anyone's intellectual property. Anyone wishing to tattle on us should direct complaints to Ryan Dancey, **ryand@organizedplay.com**. It's all part of his sinister plan ...

• Some adventure gaming modules suggest adapting situations and statistics to the capabilities of the characters in your campaign. That is fine for people who are not as smart as we are. You know who you are, Mr. Tweet, and that goes double for you, David Chart, wherever you are.

David Chart thinks he's so smart just because he knows Latin.

ou are not to alter any of the situations and
stics found in *The Sheep on the Borderlands Or:*
· I Learned to Stop Worrying and Love the Orcs.
 are not to modify the number of monsters in
m 8, you are not to fudge the ghosts' armor
s, and you are not to let anyone re-roll any dice,
od.

iolations of any ground rule will result in
REME SANCTION from the Big Game Master
he Sky (B.G.M.I.T.S., pronounced "bigamist").

ning Your Keep

ur party has journeyed for many days. You round
nd and see a shining keep in the distance. A keep,
rding to Webster's, is "the strongest, innermost
or central tower of a medieval castle; donjon."
hat last bit is included so your players are not
used by alternate meanings of the word "keep"
p the sabbath, play for keeps, and so on - because
e alternate meanings would not make any sense
is context.)
u immediately realize the keep is only there to
ide you with the opportunity to roleplay
ractions with colorful townsfolk who have
edingly creative two-syllable names like "Barak"
"Raistlin™." As a hardcore dungeon-crawler, you
very little interest in that sort of thing. Luckily,
spy a few vending machines next to a tree nearby.
h vending machine has a glass front and a slot
which gold pieces can be inserted. When an item
id for and selected, it falls into a little trough at
bottom.

he players can buy anything listed under
ponry, Armor, Goods and Services, Containers
Carriers, Special and Superior Items, and
nadelike Items from these vending machines.
se lists are all in a certain core rulebook that
remain nameless due to OGL restrictions ...
could tell you the page numbers, but we're not
wed to do that under the OGL, either, so you'll
have to thank Wizards for oppressing us so
stly.
ny time a character buys something from the
ding machine, he must roll 5d4+6. On a result
4 or less, the item gets stuck and is never going
ome out of there, no matter what. *No matter*
t.
the characters shake the vending machines and
to get random items to fall out, consult the
wing table.

The characters may want to go to the keep even
though the italicized text makes it perfectly clear
they're not supposed to and they can get all the
equipment, ale, and comely bar wenches they want
from the vending machines.

When characters try to do something they're not
supposed to, it is known as "running the GM off his
module." In the1980s, solemn roleplayers conducted
many grave seminars and earnest discussions about
what should be done when the players run the GM
off his module. Consensus was never reached
because *Vampire: The Masquerade™* was released
and suddenly everyone was much more concerned
with pretending to be invisible. If your players try
to run you off your module by pursuing an option
not explicitly described in the text of this adventure
gaming module, you should set fire to their things
until they knock it right off.

Herd the News?

You leave the vending machines behind and continue
down the path until you come to a fork in the road.
After dispensing with the inevitable tableware puns,
you set off down the trail that leads to the rest of this
adventure. Taking the second track leading off the
road and crossing the river, you take a left at the big
tree and stop at the largest boulder on the hillside.
There, next to a gently babbling brook, is your next
encounter.

Next to the babbling brook, the characters spy
Kravek the Herdsman and his flock of sheep. When
the characters approach Kravek:

Kravek the Herdsman approaches you and tells you
a long tale of woe that boils down to the fact that
three of his sheep are missing. He points in the
direction of the caves where you can find them, at
which point you accept the quest to retrieve his sheep
without engaging him in further discourse.

KRAVEK THE HERDSMAN

1st-Level Commoner (Shepherd)
Kravek is a simple herdsman
with a special fondness for sheep.
Elaboration would be both
tasteless and unnecessary.
Kravek has Mad Sheep Disease.

SHAKING THE VENDING MACHINES

2d12 - 3	RESULT
-1	lock, very simple
0 - π	saddle, exotic (military)
π - 6	iron rations*
7 - 12	dog, riding
13	bucket**
14 - 20	suit of full plate armor
21	comely bar wench

* Grievously flaunting everything sacred in *Dungeons &
Dragons®* (see the Player's Handbook, all pages), "iron
rations" were re-named "trail rations" in the third edition.
Puh-lease. This author has taken a personal vow to
continue with the old nomenclature until they pry it from
his cold, dead fingers. In retaliation for their crimes, I'd
like to note that it takes 1,000 Experience Points to make
it to 2nd level.
** This bucket is cursed. Any player touching the bucket
loses three levels. You rolled a 13, what did you expect?

Borderlands Sheep

Ovis Ammon Ariës

This is a herd of sheep.

Use the normal stats for wolverines. Instead of the wolverine's Rage special attack, which would just be silly, the borderlands sheep get the following special qualities:

Herd Mentality (Su): If one sheep can be cajoled into doing something, all of the other sheep do it as well. Because they're sheep, see.

Mad Sheep Disease (Ex): The sheep have Mad Sheep Disease. This does not cause the sheep to do anything strange, but any character who comes into contact with an infected sheep's bodily fluids must make a Constitution check, DC 12, or contract Mad Sheep Disease.

Anyone with Mad Sheep Disease must roll on the Mad Sheep Disease Symptom Table, below, every morning.

2d8+(4d6+3)-d20	Symptom
-11 - i	uncontrollable foaming at the mouth
i - 5	sex change
6 - 9	burning hands
10	burning desire
11- 12	burning pee
13	bucket*
14 - 22	carrion crawler
23 - 24	irreversible senility
25 - 29	pustules
30	heart shrinks d2 sizes that day
31 - 33	lice
34 - 37	death
38	violent spasms
39	pacifist spasms
	* See "Bucket," page XX.

The Caves of Marginal Discord

You press on in the direction of Kravek's outstretched finger and, after hacking through undergrowth for seven days, arrive in a steeply-walled valley with six different cave entrances, which we will refer to as A, B, C, D, E, and F from left to right (that is, clockwise). If you're smart you'll enter the caves starting with A and proceeding in alphabetical order, but foolhardy adventurers who want to earn the wrath of the B.G.M.I.T.S. are welcome to choose one of the other letters first.

In addition to the scripted perils, roll 2d3+2 every six turns. On a result of 6 or more, roll on the Wandering Monster Table.

Wandering Monster Table

10d2	Monster
10	tarrasque
11	bust monster (DD)
12	thirdlings
13	band of frost giants*
14	bucket**
15	owlbear
16	bugbear
17	carebear
18	black pudding***
19	turbonium dragon
20	webmaster@wizards.com

* Each frost giant carries a sack of dirty hairpin with a few rocks thrown in for good measur
** See "Bucket," page XX.
*** Entry included to satisfy Open Gaming Licen affirmative action guidelines.

Cave A: Orcs and So On

Room 1
*Just inside the entrance to this cave you s[pedestal. Resting upon it is **THE GEM ETERNAL POWER!***

Reading Note: Capped underlined bold ita indicate text to be read in a booming voice v simulated reverb.
Typographical Note for Those Consider Publishing Their Own D20 Materials Ou Their Basement: Do not try to use cap underlined bold italics at home. We're trai professionals here. Seriously.

Gem of Eternal Power Trap (CR 2(

Anyone who touches the legendary Gem Eternal Power is crushed to death (no sav by the giant boulder that hangs above th pedestal (no chance to detect or disable). Th Gem of Eternal Power is made of worthle glass, and is crushed, too.
So ha ha on the players.

Rooms 2 - 11
Pressing on, you discover the Hall of Infi Orcs.*

No character may leave this set of rooms impenetrable force field prevents it - unti orcs are slain, even the women and child *Especially* the women and children. This course, is impossible, considering that eac these rooms contains a number of orcs ec to the number of the room times infinit
So double ha ha on the players.
While the characters fight the orcs,

embodied voices of John Wick and Gary
'gax® debate the ethics of the wholesale
termination of various goblinoid races. John
ck eventually strangles Gary Gygax®, and good
dance, but it is too late for the orcs that have
eady been killed.

One of the orcs inexplicably runs around
puting: "BREE-YARK!" He was a candidate for
dership of the tribe who was passed over when
ess-qualified woman applied for the position.
you don't have the stats for orcs memorized, you're
ding the wrong adventure gaming module, bucko.
The number of the room is also inlaid in the middle
the floor in polished marble.

ve B: Ghosts

he walls of the tunnels here have been polished
ooth and glow with yellow light. In the middle
the tunnel ahead of you, a single electrum piece
ats in the air about three feet off the ground.
ere's another one ten feet up the tunnel. And
other, and another…

Each of the little dots on the map indicates a
ating electrum piece. The big dots indicate
ating wheels of cheese. Eating a cheese wheel
e entire thing must be consumed) gives the
lity to automatically kill the ghosts that inhabit
s maze by biting them. This ability lasts d%-
(20+20) rounds.

om 1

This room contains four ghosts. When the
aracters pass through the cave entrance, the
osts come out of this room one at a time and
nder the passages randomly until they meet
with the player characters, at which point they
ack.

GHOSTS (4)

1ulti-Level Maze-Dwelling Apparitions
Each ghost has the vague shape of a round-
osed bullet standing on end, with a ragged
ottom edge, and has googly
yes that point in the
host's direction of
ravel. Each of the four
s a different solid
olor: red, blue, yellow,
nd white. Their names
re Blinky™, Pinky™,
nky™, and Clyde™.

Use the stats for the
arrasque … when a player meets up with one
f these guys, game over! Each ghost also has
he following special quality:
lash Blue When Cheese Is Consumed (Su):
he ghosts flash with an eerie blue light when
 player eats one of the wheels of cheese. This
sts for 1d6 rounds, and doesn't ever help the
layer in any significant way.

Cave C: Stirges

A large cavern lit by many flaming torches.
Dozens of dwarves eat potatoes and corn. Their
riding hogs are parked in neat rows along the edges
of the cave. One of the dwarves finishes slamming
an ale, approaches you, and says: "Welcome! We're
here for Stirges!"

STIRGES DWARVES

3rd-Level (Road) Warriors
These dwarves dress in black
leather armor painted
with oaths and pictures.
None wear helmets,
and they mock any
character who wears
a helmet for being a
"big pussy." They
have the following
new skills:
Skills: Ride Hog +12, Tinker with Hog +6

HOG, RIDING

Greased Lightnin'
Each hog has a leather saddle and seems
content to stand in a row with its brethren until
mounted. It is relatively easy to knock a standing
hog over (Strength check DC 10),
which results in a chain reaction
that knocks the entire row to
the ground. Unlucky or
clumsy characters might
do this by accident.
Tipping a row of hogs
really pisses off the dwarves.
Use the normal stats for
boars, just to be different. The hogs all have the
following special quality:
Produce Loud Noise (Ex): Hogs are very noisy
when in motion.

A NOTE FROM THE ARS MAGICA™ SOCIETY

Motto: *Haec est sententia nostra, sed Latine.*
We object to the use of potatoes and corn
in this adventure gaming module. The
vegetables in question were not discovered
until Europeans visited the New World in the
fifteenth century, and therefore could not be
possessed by dwarves in this location in this
time period. Furthermore, we are outraged
by the recent television adaptation of Homer's
Odyssey, and would like to take this
opportunity to re-state, in the strongest
possible terms, our objection that the Perdo
Ignem™ spells in the fourth edition should be
about ten levels higher than they are.
Explanatory Note: We were sued and forced
to put this bit in. These *Ars Magica*™ players
have way too much time on their hands.

Cave D: The Best Cave Yet

You enter this cave complex and discover that in order to plumb its depths and secure the wondrous treasures located herein, you must purchase adventure gaming module TSOTB2, available from Atlas Games for a very reasonable price.

Cave E: Sponsored by the Letter E

You enter an enormous cave containing egg-plants, Edgar Allen Poe, Ecuadorians, eels, Earp (Wyatt), estrogen, ents, elbows, ErnieTM (of Sesame StreetTM), ElleTM (the magazine, not the letter), exfoliant, emeralds, and the biggest erstwhile you ever saw.

Suddenly, [the character who has irritated the Game Master most recently] realizes that [a prized possession of his that begins with the letter E] is missing from his [pouch/bag/pocket]. [A second character known to be perceptive] hears a faint [noise] and sees a/an [adjective] flicker as an Ethereal Filcher disappears from sight.

The materials in this cave, which, as noted above, has been sponsored by the letter E, have been collected by Elmer the Educated, an Ethereal Filcher from the East End of Esbjerg,* over many years of living in this cave. He continues adding to his collection as long as the characters stay here and continue possessing items that begin with the letter E.

* FYI: Esbjerg is a seaport in Denmark. Its population is approximately 81,000.

ELMER
Educated Ethereal Filcher from the East End of Esbjerg

One day, back when Elmer was known as Walter, he ran across an Elven philosopher who was drunk out of his mind. Said philosopher managed to convince Walter that E was the best of all possible letters, thus setting into motion events leading to the characters' encounter with him in a cave sponsored by the letter E. (And you thought there was no conceivable in-game reason for a cave full of things that start with E!)

Elmer will not steal from elves; he respects them too much. He would very much like to meet an elemental. Especially an earth elemental. For obvious reasons. Elmer can speak Esperanto, and would love to have a philosophical discourse in that language.

Use the normal stats for an Ethereal Filcher; Or don't. See if I care.

Languages: Esperanto

Cave F: The Big Finale

You enter a series of six square rooms, each with a number of pillars in it. Touching one of the pillars turns you to stone, even if you use a ten-foot pole, so you'll probably want to avoid doing that.

As you look around in the eerie light that seems to

emanate from the putrid green stuff attached to of the walls, you see a sheep stealthily darting thro one of the doorways, just out of sight.

The characters, presumably, give chase, whic fine. It's to be expected, really, the point of scenario being to catch the sheep and return t to Kravek. (That is to say, catching sheep is the p of this scenario in addition to mocking gam products, personalities, and conventions. An(conventions I refer, of course, to the "customs formalities" of gaming, not to the gathering players of games organized by half-witted col gaming clubs who need to spend their portio the university's onerous student fees on *someth* But I digress. Which is of no matter, as I am b(paid by the word.)

Because of a magical enchantment (for w Michelle A. Brown Nephew will make up necessary game statistics at a later date – www.atlas-games.com for corrections to this numerous other "artistic decisions"), it is imposs for the characters to catch any of the sheep be two conditions are fulfilled. They must e; individually:
1) Stop Worrying
2) Learn to Love the Orcs

Luckily, the sheep speak the Common tongu any of the characters think to ask the sheep wh attempts to catch them work no matter what, of the three can inform the characters of the sheep-catching requirements. They can even sug activities that would sufficiently demonst accomplishment of the conditions.

SAMPLE ACTIVITIES TO DEMONSTRA1 ONE HAS STOPPED WORRYING

- Speak in a Jamaican accent about su(subjects as ganja and Bob Marle
- If you meet the Buddha, kill the Buddh
- Search out an individual named "Worryin(and thwart his plans. Whatever they ar
- Touch one of the pillars on purpos
- Abandon quest to find sheep and lea\ Borderlands.

SAMPLE ACTIVITIES TO DEMONSTRAT ONE HAS LEARNED TO LOVE THE ORC (AND THAT ARE NOT PORNOGRAPHIC

- Kiss an orc.
- Have pages 146 and 147 of the Monst Manual laminated so they'll never get musse
- Dress like an orc. Of the opposite gender. A be obvious about liking it.
- Write a song to the tune of "Rainbc Connection" that demonstrates honest a abiding concern about the plight of the orci race.
- Mail five dollars to Jeff Tidball, care of Do Tower. He'll make sure it gets to an orci charity for you.

Once every member of the party has stopped worrying and learned to love the orcs, Larry, Curly, and Moe (the sheep) agree to come with them back to Kravek the Herdsmen, and thus, everything comes full circle. Full enough circle, anyway.

Larry, Curly, and Moe

0th-Level Rogue Sheep

Use the statistics for borderlands sheep, except add Evasion, Uncanny Dodge, Slippery Mind, and Sneak Attack +5d6.

Very Difficult to Catch (Su): You can't catch the sheep until you Stop Worrying and Learn to Love the Orcs.

Language: Common

Wrapping Up

When the PCs return the rogue sheep, Kravek the Herdsman gives them 350,000 gp.* Use the following formula to determine how many experience points each character gets:

Experience Points = 2p2 + (2a ± x)

An extensive survey of online D20 product reviews determined that this is, indeed, the optimal reward for a party of 1st-level characters.

Special Bonus

You can cut out Cave F, fold it up, and make it into a six-sided die! Whoo-hoo!

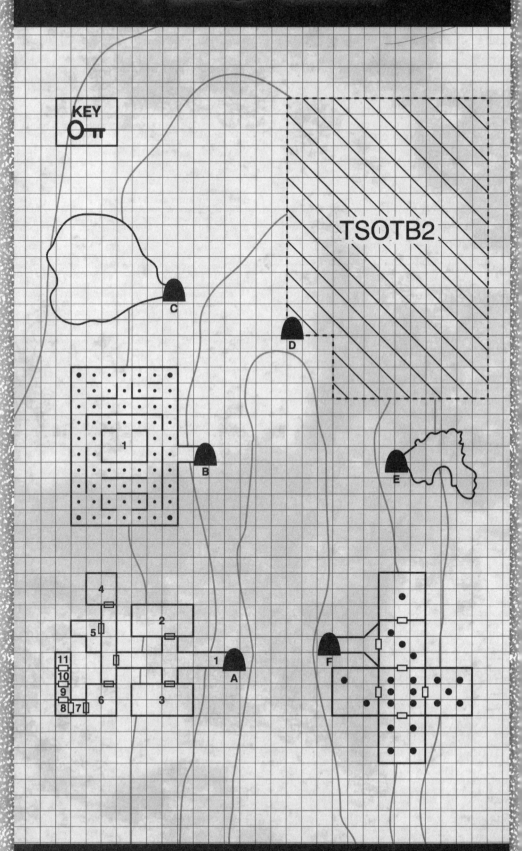

PENUMBRA

KEY

TSOTB2

Afterward
by Jolly Blackburn

LONG AGO, IN A WORLD NOT SO FAR AWAY (OKAY, MAYBE IT WASN'T ALL THAT LONG AGO EITHER) THERE EXISTED A WORLD OF DORKS AND GEEKS FILLED WITH MANY QUESTIONS.

"WHO ARE WE?"

"WHY ARE WE HERE?"

"WHO TOOK THE LAST PIECE OF PIZZA?"

"DUDE, ARE YOU SURE THAT'S YOUR TWENTY-SIDER? I'M MISSING MINE."

THEN ONE DAY A TOWER WAS ROSE UP TO LOOM OVER THE LANDSCAPE. AS THE GEEKS AND DORKS GATHERED AROUND TO MARVEL AT THIS NEW ADDITION TO THEIR WORLD, A STRANGE FIGURE EMERGED FROM WITHIN.

"HELLO!" HE SAID, "I'M JOHN. AND THIS IS DORK TOWER. WIPE YOUR SHOES AND COME ON IN. I THINK I HAVE SOME ANSWERS FOR THOSE QUESTIONS THAT HAVE BEEN NAGGING YOU."

AND SO THE MOB ENTERED. THEY DINED. THEY WINED. THEY BUSTED OUT THE GOOD COMFY CHAIR. AND AS THE SUN BEGAN TO SET AND THE EVENING DREW LONG – THEY STAYED. FOR THEY DISCOVERED THAT BEING A DORK WAS ACTUALLY PRETTY KEWL. MORE IMPORTANTLY, THEY DISCOVERED THEY WERE IN GOOD COMPANY.

DORK TOWER HAS BEEN MY FAVORITE COMIC (WELL, AHEM, SECOND FAVORITE) SINCE I LAID EYES ON THE VERY FIRST ISSUE.

JOHN UNDERSTANDS US BECAUSE HE'S ONE OF US. WE SEE OURSELVES AND OUR FRIENDS THROUGH HIS EYES AND WE LIKE WHAT WE SEE.

Jolly R. Blackburn

VICE PRESIDENT, KENZERCO
CHICAGO, IL.
3/28/02

About the Author

John Kovalic was born in Manchester, England, in 1962. Dork Tower began in SHADIS magazine in 1996, and the Origins award-winning Dork Tower comic book was launched in June 1998. The first issue sold out in eight weeks to fantastic reviews and tremendous industry buzz. John's award-winning editorial cartoons appear everywhere from his hometown WISCONSIN STATE JOURNAL and CAPITAL TIMES (Madison, WI) to the NEW YORK TIMES and the WASHINGTON POST. His other creations include SnapDragons and Newbies  (with Liz Rathke), Wild Life, Beached, the Unspeakable Oaf and many others.

One of the first cartoonists to put their work on the internet, his self-produced World Wide Web site, kovalic.com, has received numerous national and international kudos. If you ask him nicely, he'll tell you how he helped create GAMES Magazine's 1999 Party Game of the Year, the international best-selling, award-winning "Apples to Apples." He may even tell you how he once ended up in the pages of the National Enquirer.

His degree was in Economics with a minor in Astrophysics. In his spare time, John searches for spare time.